THE
Compost Book

THE
Compost Book

David & Yvonne Taylor

ILLUSTRATED BY

Helen McCosker

ROBERT HALE • LONDON

© *David and Yvonne Taylor 1993*
Illustrations © Helen McCosker 1993
First published in Great Britain 1994

ISBN 0 7090 5464 5

Robert Hale Limited
Clerkenwell House
Clerkenwell Green
London EC1R 0HT

2 4 6 8 10 9 7 5 3 1

Edited by Louise Egerton

Designed by Robert Taylor

Illustrations by Helen McCosker

Typeset in Australia by Deblaere Typesetting Pty Ltd

Produced by Mandarin Offset

Printed in Hong Kong

"Lilacs out of

the

dead land"

THE WASTELAND
– T.S. ELLIOT

How to use
this book

*We have tried to design
this book for quick reference, so you can
dip in and out of it, finding facts
and solving problems. To obtain
a fundamental grip on what compost is
all about, we suggest you read the
introductory section and the following
key entries in the A to Z section first:
Elements, Accelerators, Animal
manure, Micro-organisms, NPK,
Nutrients, pH and Temperature.
Then take a look at the handy
Carbon/Nitrogen Cone*

and the Uses and Values Table at the
back of the book. You will probably
find yourself coming back to these
frequently once you begin composting.
Where words appear in bold in the
A to Z section, they constitute an entry
in their own right and may serve to
broaden a subject out. A quick
checklist of all entries can be found on
page 15. Letters appearing in brackets
following an entry name are the
chemical symbol for that element.

Introduction

Welcome to the world of waste and worms. Many wastes around us are useful and free, so gather up those grass clippings, tear up your newspapers, save your fruit and vegetable peelings and your tea leaves. You are about to declare war on waste and want by composting just about everything. You will be amazed to discover how much so-called garbage can be recycled to make compost. Compost-making works well as long as you understand its requirements and reactions. A compost heap can be a sad mess, like a failed sponge cake, so read on, follow our recipes, add accelerators and leaf through the

A to Z pages of this book where we have tried to solve the mysteries of compost production.
Here you will find out what can and cannot be composted, whether to encourage or discourage the living things haunting your heap and all about bins, boxes, tumblers, shredders and munchers. You will learn about the varying potency of certain manures and about some useful properties of herbs in the heap. You will discover how to apply compost to flowerbeds, shrubs and fruit trees and how to use it as a potting or seedling mix. We hope this little book inspires you to action, leading to heaps of happy composting.

What Is Compost?

Compost is a fundamental plant food. It feeds the soil from which all your plants draw their goodness. After a season of fruiting, flowering and vegetable production, a natural way to revitalize your tired old soil is with an application of well prepared compost. Plants grown in these freshly composted beds will flourish in an abundance of bright colours and green leaves; their strength will deter most pests, too.

All You Need to Know About Compost

It is important that your compost heap or bin is not treated simply as a dump. Composting is a biochemical process, a form of digestion in fact. Like any digestive system it needs a balanced diet if it is to perform well. So balance is the key to a good compost.

Your compost needs 16 elements, 10 of them only in small (trace) quantities. The other 6, however, are major contributors, especially nitrogen and carbon which exist in all organic matter. To maintain a healthy balance between these two elements, consult the Carbon/Nitrogen Cone at the back of the book. You will see that materials such as grass clippings, hay, straw or sawdust must be added in much greater quantities than kitchen and garden wastes. For instance one container of kitchen waste needs ten containers of grass clippings to balance it.

A moisture balance and an alkalinity/acidity balance are also important. These are not hard to maintain. Your compost should be moist but not sodden. During wet weather cover it with a lid or plastic sheeting. To test the acidity/alkalinity, consult the pH scale given on page 62.

The other vital aspect of good compost-making lies with millions of micro-organisms. Two types are needed in your heap to convert the waste materials to compost. One, anaerobic bacteria, function in the airless conditions inside the heap. The other, aerobic bacteria, need oxygen. These micro-organisms are the driving force in the whole composting process. Both are essential.

How To Make Compost

There are two production methods, fast and not so fast.

FAST COMPOSTS can be made in a heap or a tumbler. Careful preparation is essential. Chop ingredients with a spade and be sure to include plentiful amounts of 'digesting' materials, such as grass clippings. See **recipes** for combinations and quantities of materials. Mix everything well and keep the mixture moist. Add substances to speed the fermentation process: these are listed in the book under **accelerators**.

If a tumbler is used, turn every day. In as little as nine days your compost may be ready to use.

If making compost in a heap, keep it compact. After two or three days the fermentation should be well under way in the centre of the heap, so at this point toss and turn it every third day. At the end of two weeks the compost should be mature and ready for use.

NOT-SO-FAST COMPOSTS can be made in bins or boxes; three are needed to provide ongoing amounts of mature compost. Materials should be in the same proportions as for fast composts and the addition of a layer of manure from time to time is beneficial. Keep covered against heavy rain.

This is a low maintenance method and no turning is necessary, but each collection will take three months or more to mature. To enrich the mixture and to speed it up a little add accelerators and **additives**.

Whatever type of compost you make, once mature apply it as soon as possible. When it is left standing in the open for a long period, nutrients seep away in the rain and are lost to the air as vapours.

Why Make Fast Composts?

We favour composts that are made quickly, so you can revitalize your garden continuously, even if composting space is limited. We have included in this book a quick compost recipe developed by David which we call Fast Fourteen. It contains all the nutrients that plants need and is ready for use in two weeks. We hope you will try it and reap the benefits, as we have.

Confusing Terms

Just a word about the terms compost, manure, fertilizer and mulch. There is often some confusion about what is meant by each of these.

Compost is a natural fertilizer and, if its contents are right, it should contain all the nutrients that plants need.

Manure is a perfect form of compost produced in the digestive system of grazing animals. It is a fertilizer.

Chemically manufactured artificial fertilizers contain the elements that plants need. They are designed to force feed the plants, and are soluble in soil fluids. They leave no nutrients for the next crop and destroy soil organisms, such as earthworms, which are essential to healthy soil.

Mulch is a mat of dead plant material such as hay. It conserves moisture in the soil and protects plants and trees against extreme temperatures, wind and excessive rain. It is not a fertilizer.

Contents

Accelerators

Compost accelerators speed up microbiological activity and so the decomposition process (see **Temperature**). Fresh animal manures, grass clippings, liquid manure, seaweed extract, bran, molasses and yeast are all accelerators; so also are the herbs borage, comfrey, dandelion, stinging nettle and yarrow.

Commercial compost accelerators are available and, judging from their listed ingredients, are no doubt effective, but you can make up your own for a fraction of the cost.

Here's one good recipe: make a hole in the compost heap and fill it with 5 parts grass clippings to 1 part fresh manure. Sprinkle with bran. Add 40 ml of seaweed extract and 250 ml of molasses to 10 litres of warm water. Mix well and pour mixture into the hole. Cover with more compost material. It is cheapest to buy your bran and molasses from bulk health food stores and to take your own container for the molasses.

Acidity/Alkalinity

See **pH**.

Additives

Additives are minerals that supplement the nutrient content of a compost and speed up decomposition.

They may be mineral **chelates**—as with the iron in stinging nettles and dandelion; the calcium, phosphate and potassium in comfrey leaves; or the array of nutrient minerals in seaweed and to a lesser extent molasses. The enzymes in these substances activate and accelerate the fermentation process whilst at the same time rapidly releasing the mineral supplements.

Additives may also be derived from wood ash,

soot, bone meal and from rock flours and dusts. Rock supplements include calcium in limestone, calcium and magnesium in dolomite, phosphorus in phosphate rock and guano and potassium-rich granites and basalts. These rock substances tend to be 'slow release' additives, so add sparingly. Some of them are not easy to obtain but dolomite is available in small quantities from garden centres and in larger quantities from potters' suppliers.

Air

Air is essential to the composting process as it supplies oxygen for the aerobic (oxygen-absorbing) bacteria, which stimulate fermentation, glucose production and the fixing of nitrogen.

Anaerobic bacteria

Inside the heap, where there is no air, anaerobic bacteria develop, forming sulphur compounds which smell like rotten eggs and ammonia. They heat the heap—an essential part of the decomposing process—and concentrate essential nutrients. Toss and turn the compost every third day, and the aerobic and anaerobic organisms will flourish alternately. Keep the heap moist. See also **Temperature**.

Animal manures

The best manures are produced by vegetarian animals. The grasses, grains and other vegetable matter are digested while the waste material is 'composted' within the animal in a perfect way. Once this waste is excreted, the aerobic (oxygen-absorbing) bacteria accelerate the composting process still further and the smell disappears.

Meat-eating animals produce very small amounts of manure compared to grazing animals. Excreta from dogs and cats may contain parasites and should not be added to composts.

Manures can be kept in either plastic bags or in a covered heap. While fresh manure added to a compost heap will maximize its potency, only well-matured animal manures should be applied directly to soil. Manure is mature and ready for use when inhabited by earthworms. Their presence implies that the temperature is reasonable, aeration is good, moisture balanced and acidity/alkalinity neutral.

When applying manure to established trees, fork it around the drip line (where water drips from the outermost leaves).

Each type of manure has different qualities and contributes to particular functions within a plant. For more information, see **Chicken, Pigeon, Cow, Goat, Duck, Sheep** and **Horse manure**.

Ants

A dry compost heap can become an ant heap but no harm will be done. The ants will redistribute all the material, so the heap will not need to be tossed. The day before using ant-infested compost, water it well and the ants will leave.

Application of compost

When the temperature in your compost has dropped to the maximum daily air temperature, it is ready for use. If your compost has undergone sufficient heating, no seed will grow from it, but if you are sowing seed directly into it and you want to be absolutely sure, you can put it in the freezer for a couple of days. Compost covering sown seed should be sieved and well compacted.

When applying compost to flowerbeds, dig it in lightly with the existing soil. If the compost is mature, there should be no risk of it burning small plants, so don't worry if it touches the stalks.

Established shrubs and fruit trees will benefit from a ring of compost. Fork it in around the drip line, where water drips from the outermost leaves. Sprinkle this ring with dolomite and cover with a mulch of hay, straw or dried grass clippings. The fine roots will benefit from this as they grow outward and the ground will retain moisture in hot or windy weather. For direct planting into compost, see **Strip trenching**.

Bacteria

These micro-organisms are by far the most abundant living matter in soil. They break down plant and animal residues in the compost, thereby releasing carbon dioxide, which plants absorb as gaseous vapours. Another vital role of bacteria is to convert organic nitrogen into ammonia and finally nitrates, which plants can then absorb through water. One group of bacteria fix nitrogen in the root nodules of legumes.

See also **Anaerobic bacteria**.

Berries, brambles and roses

Residues from making jams, jellies amd syrups are quickly composted. The thorny canes will disintegrate if munched in a shredder or chopped with a sharpened blade. Cover the canes with soil or carpet underfelt with added compost or animal manure. In a few months this heap will be ready to grow an abundance of cucurbits – courgettes, marrows or squash.

Bins and boxes

The essential features of a compost bin or box are holes in the sides for air to enter and access for worms and other earth organisms at the base. Place boxes or bins on the soil. Very simple styles have advantages; a circle of wire mesh can be made in minutes and when filled with compacted materials, lifted clear to start again. Cardboard cartons with a large hole in the base and holes cut in the sides provide a series of neat compost containers and they will eventually break down. Worms love cardboard.

More elaborate boxes can be made from bricks or timber. All compost containers should be covered on top.

Composting bins are available commercially and some municipal authorities are selling bins cheaply to encourage household composting.

Blood and bone

This is a commercial by-product of slaughterhouses and butchers. Rich in phosphorus and nitrogen, bones have been a fertilizer source for centuries. During the nineteenth century Britain was accused of 'grave robbing' the battlefields of Europe in order to sustain her agriculture.

Today the bones are ground, dried blood added and a meal produced. Blood and bone can be extended by composting it with fibrous materials such as sawdust, lawn clippings or hay, or it can be applied directly onto soil, but be careful to sprinkle it away from young plants as it may 'burn' them.

Many organic gardeners consider this to be an unhealthy product and avoid using it. It is possible that residues of chemical products and antibiotics remain in the blood and bone meal and are harmful to micro-organisms.

Borage

A herb closely related to comfrey, it is also of great value to the compost as it develops massive succulent stalks, with many leaves and flowers. Chop with a spade and add to your heap.

Boron (B)

Boron plays a vital role in flowering and fruiting. **Seawater** contains high levels of boron which is concentrated in **seaweed**. Boron deficiency reduces the intake of other nutrient elements by the plants, which then become degenerate.

Bran

Bran is the residue from refining or polishing wheat, rice or other grains. Bran contains a number of vitamins and enzymes and is a good source of **NPK** nutrients as well as iron.

It is an excellent compost **accelerator** but bees will swarm over it if it is left uncovered. No doubt this is proof of its nutritional value. Bran is used as a poultry food and is available cheaply from health food stores.

Calcium (Ca)

Calcium ensures plant maturity, high seed production and the intake of other essential elements. Although it occurs in relative abundance in the Earth's crust, calcium is in short supply or absent in soils derived purely from porous sandstone. If your soil should need a calcium supplement, add ground limestone or preferably ground dolomite, which also helps adjust soil acidity by acting as a **liming** agent.

Carbon and carbon dioxide (C and CO_2)

Carbon atoms are the cornerstones of all molecules within plants. They form carbohydrates and the fibrous substance called cellulose. Carbon contributes about 44% of dry plant material and is absorbed by plants in the gaseous form, carbon dioxide.

The decomposition of organic matter by the action of micro-organisms generates carbon dioxide. The carbon dioxide in turn fuels—or feeds—bacterial conversion of cellulose into glucose, which again produces carbon dioxide. This is an almost self-perpetuating system which is on-going in compost-making. As large amounts of carbon dioxide escape into the atmosphere, it is preferable to restrict air to the compost heap at times with a cover.

When carbon dioxide is incorporated in water it forms a weak acid, carbonic acid. This acid dissolves soil-borne nutrients from humus, clay and mineral grains, making them ready for absorption by plants.

Carbon-Nitrogen balance

All organic matter contains both carbon and nitrogen in varying proportions. A vital function of composting is to convert carbon and nitrogen into plant food. The carbon content needs to be 25 times greater than the nitrogen content by weight but should not be more than 30 times greater. This optimum ratio can be achieved by referring to **The Carbon/Nitrogen Cone** at the back of the book.

If there is too much carbon there will be a rapid production of carbon dioxide, which will burn out the material before the nitrogen is converted biologically into ammonia. The resulting compost will be greatly reduced in volume, light in colour and nutrient deficient.

Too little carbon inhibits the production of biological energy in the heap, slowing the decomposing process. A dark, smelly mess results. A varied diet is essential for your compost to become humus-rich, nitrogenous and friable.

Cardboard

Cardboard is a good mulching material but it needs a lot of dry material or compost on top to hold it in place until it is well soaked with water. It can also be composted, at the bottom of a heap or packed around the sides of a bin.

Worms love corrugated cardboard, so it must have good food value.

Carpet underfelt

Carpet layers will give you off-cuts of new underfelt
and discarded old felt. Only those of natural fibre will
decompose. Test the composition with a lighted
match: if the threads melt then the felt is synthetic.

Underfelt can be used in various ways and when
it finally breaks down it is a natural soil component.
As a cover over a compost heap or box, it helps the
heating and fermentation inside the heap, or use it to
mulch around trees to keep weeds down and reduce
evaporation.

A freshly composted garden bed can be covered
with underfelt. To plant out seedlings cut holes in the
felt and plant directly into the compost beneath. To

sow seed, cut slits and lay a fine layer of compost in the slits. This is a water- and nutrient-retaining system, particularly good in sandy, coastal or arid inland soils.

Cartons

Milk and other drink cartons can be composted but they take a long time—many months. Their only residue is a fine film of plastic from the outside. But they are a nuisance in a compost heap, so give them a small corner of their own with some leaves or grass clippings on top. It is very satisfying when they finally disintegrate.

Cartons are also good for seed planting. When the seedlings are ready to plant out, cut the bottom of the carton away and put the rest in the soil or under mulch. In this way the seedling is not disturbed and the carton will weather away.

Chamomile

Rich in calcium, chamomile is a good additive to compost and it subdues smells, keeping the compost sweet. The herb is worth growing as it is known as the plant doctor, helping many plants and the soil to keep healthy.

Charcoal

Charcoal is a residue from wood fires. It is mineral rich and so of value in compost. It can be separated from wood ash in water, since charcoal floats. It is a very porous material and acts like a sponge for nutrients dissolved in water. If you leave charcoal in a **liquid manure or tea**, for example, it will act as a slow-release plant food when incorporated in garden beds.

Charcoal is also a valuable addition to potting mix, improving drainage and aeration, as well as being a nutrient source. Plant roots seek out this enrichment and can be seen growing into the charcoal.

Chelates (pronounced Kee-lates)

Chelates are organic compounds which have attracted inorganic metals into their structures. Chelate means claw-like and this gives a picture of the process. In bonding with stable organic substances, the metallic element becomes available in the soil for plant absorption.

Our own health also requires chelated elements.

We cannot cure anaemia by swallowing iron filings. Even our absorption of iron from various inorganic salts is pitifully slow but when iron is bonded into organic amino acid compounds, rapid absorption takes place.

grass or compost

dark soil

COMPACTED iRON-riCH NuTRieNt-pOOR LAyER

Mineral elements in the soil are congregated by chelation with organic compounds. This applies particularly to the **trace elements** iron, copper, boron and manganese. Chelates are water soluble and stable and so are readily converted into plant tissue.

Composting produces chelates. Earthworms and all organic material added to the soil have chelating properties. Mosses and lichens attached to apparently barren rocks survive by producing chelating substances which dissolve rocks to release micro-nutrients. This chelating mechanism permits lichen to grow in such hostile environments as ice-free rock surfaces in the Antarctic.

Foods such as **molasses, yeast, yoghurt and buttermilk** are rich in a wide range of chelated mineral nutrients and are thus excellent compost additives and accelerators.

To see how iron may be chelated from the soil by compost or mulch, see **Iron**.

Chicken manure

Chicken manure contains a good balance of **NPK** nutrients. All bird excreta is highly concentrated as the nitrogen-rich urea is combined with the solids and not voided as a liquid.

The high phosphate content is excellent for fruiting vegetables, such as tomatoes, but the manure must not be applied fresh, as ammonia is given off and will harm plants.

Mature fresh chicken manure in a heap, covered with soil or vegetable matter to conserve valuable nitrates. When worms invade the heap the manure is mature. This should take less than a month. Bird droppings lack roughage, so to retain moisture mix with hay, sawdust or shredded paper.

The domestic hen is an efficient producer of compost when housed on deep litter and fed on vegetable scraps and grain. This litter of hay or straw is turned constantly by the bird, which each year gives 10 kg of manure and, of course, eggs. For suburban gardens, bustling little bantams are ideal and make very charming pets. Kept on deep litter, there are almost no smells or flies.

Pelletized poultry manure is commercially available. Another poultry manure, **Dynamic Lifter**, has an excellent reputation. It is a concentrated organic fertilizer, produced by a composting method. It is processed under chemically controlled conditions so that the ammonia compounds are converted into benign nitrates with concentrations of other nutrients and trace elements.

Chlorine (Cl)

Although it is an essential trace element, chlorine is seldom lacking in soil as vegetation and rainfall supply a sufficiency.

Clover

Clover is a spreading **legume** which fixes **nitrogen** and acts as a **living mulch**, retaining moisture in the soil and inhibiting weed growth. Red and white clovers can be sown from seed and are available from health food stores. When grown, the clover can be cut and added to the compost, either as a **green manure** or dried as a hay. The roots, left in position, enrich the soil with nitrogen.

The 'Clever Clover' technique was developed in Australia as a weed control measure. In spring or summer strips can be dug or holes cut so the seed, seedlings or bulbs can be planted into the 'Fertile Mat'. Clover seed is available from John Chambers Wild Flower Seeds and Chiltern Seeds (see **Living mulch**).

Coffee grounds

These are high in proteins and oils, which makes them good micro-organism food—perfect for the compost. Don't apply them directly to growing plants as they will wilt with the rancid aroma.

In the industrial process, after the essentials are

extracted from coffee beans to produce instant coffee, the residues become waste. If you can, get a quantity of this waste from a factory.

Comfrey

The succulent leaves of this herb are rich in calcium, phosphorus, potassium and vitamins A, C and B12. Chop the leaves with a spade and add them to the heap. Alternatively, make a liquid tea with them and apply it directly to your soil, diluted with 5 parts water.
See also **Liquid manures and teas**.

Compost water

This is an excellent fertilizer for house plants and for revitalizing soil. Simply soak a quantity of mature compost in water for an hour or two. Pour off the liquid, which can be readily absorbed by plant roots, diluting it if it seems necessary. Add more water to the same compost several times for use in this way, then use the spent compost residue as a mulch.

Contaminants and pollutants

If the sources of composting materials are unknown they may contain contaminants. These may inhibit the biological activity, which is so essential to the satisfactory maturation of the compost, and affect the vegies to be grown in it.
Contaminants and pollutants can be inorganic substances, such as sulphur, lead or cadmium. See **Paper, Sulphur**, and **Trace elements**.
The major concern, however, is with toxic organics: insecticides, herbicides and fungicides. These may be present as residues in a range of plant wastes,

sawdust, hay and straw. Animal manures from factory farming may contain such residues and, in addition, the effects from hormone and antibiotic treatments may upset microbial action in compost.

On the positive side of all this is the fact that composting will break down many of these substances. If the earthworms keep away from a mature compost, then there is a problem.

You don't always know what you are bringing into your garden. In our community garden hundreds of bags of grass clippings were received each year from a mowing contractor. These were emptied into a heap on their own and many bags had a strong chemical smell. The heap was tossed every two or three days and the chemical smell quickly diminished. After only eight to ten days the resulting dark, friable material was used as a mulch without any ill effects to the plants.

Cooking oils and fats

Since these are organic, they will compost. It is best to pour them into a hole in your compost and cover to avoid flies, etc.

Copper (Cu)

Copper is present in a number of enzymes and probably plays a catalytic role in plant respiration and utilization of iron. It can be maintained at the desired level by applications of grass clippings, sawdust or seaweed to the compost.

Cow manure

Cattle are very efficient digesters of vegetation, especially fibrous grasses and hay. Their composting vessel is known as a rumen. Here food is worked over by myriad bacteria and other micro-organisms.

Cellulose is reduced by enzymal action to a pulp and regurgitated for a further chewing. It then passes through the true stomach for final digestion. This is a highly adapted and efficient cellulose-splitting system and takes eighteen days to complete.

The fresh manure contains nutrients and an array of micro-organisms. Their function changes when the anaerobic environment within the animal is exchanged for the aerobic state of the paddock.

The whole digestive and elimination process is so efficient that little of the food taken in by the beast is passed out as manure, but because it is rich in both micro-organisms and enzymes cow manure is very beneficial in compost and is an excellent worm food. It also makes a valuable liquid manure.

Pelletized cow manure is available commercially. The product has been kiln dried and it is not clear whether the enzymes and bacteria can be revitalized when water is added to reconstitute the manure.

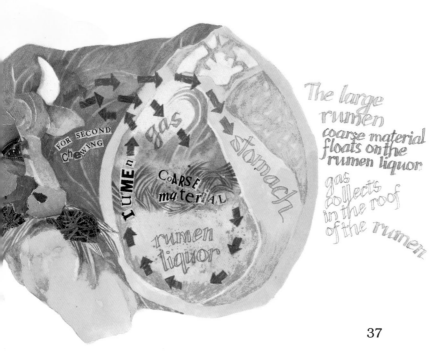

Dandelion

In their growing process, dandelions absorb two to three times more iron than any other plant. Iron is a trace element and also an activator. Dandelions can be added as whole plants or as a liquid tea.

Dolomite

Dolomite aids biochemical processes in plant growth. It is a rock that usually has been formed in shallow seas or estuaries. It is not only a liming material and a soil conditioner, but it is a contributor of calcium and magnesium to the soil.

Because it is formed in sea water it also contains other vital concentrated trace elements, such as manganese, boron and iron. As leached soil types are deficient in these nutrients, dolomite provides an excellent supplement to the soil or to a mature compost.

Application of dolomite is essential for growing fruit and vegetables on porous sandstone soils, such as those around estuaries. Citrus trees benefit if dolomite is added to compost, mulch or manure being spread around them.

Duck manure

This manure is rich in nitrogen and phosphorus, so it is a very valuable product. The sloppy nature of the manure and the tendency of the birds to 'duck under' fences and gates and go travelling makes duck-keeping a difficult proposition in suburban gardens.

Dynamic Lifter

See **Chicken manure**.

Earthworms

The earthworms in your compost feed on vegetable and animal refuse and expel casts. These casts are a valuable manure on their own. They contain micro-organisms, rich in **NPK** and other nutrients, and are bound together by biochemically complex mucus. Remarkably, trace elements not discernible in your soil, may be present in worm casts in that soil. Worm casts are even marketed as a liquid manure (see **Liquid manures and teas**).

Earthworms are reliable indicators of pollution. If

earthworms keep away from compost materials which have been kept moist and covered for some weeks, the heap contains something toxic.

If your garden is totally lacking in earthworms, they can be ordered by mail from worm farms.

Famed for his controversial work *On the Origin of Species*, Charles Darwin did valuable fieldwork on earthworms, over a period of many years. He wrote, 'it may be doubted whether there are any other animals which have played so important a part in the history of the world...'. He described them as 'Nature's ploughshare' and concluded that all the vegetable mould in England has passed and will pass, time and time again, through the intestinal tract of earthworms.

Eggshells

Eggshells break down quickly and provide lime to a compost. Also the membrane inside the shell contains a complexity of organic molecules on which bacteria multiply once the shell is broken. Organic acids from nitrogenous material dissolve the alkaline eggshells, which in turn neutralize the acids.

Elements

Sixteen elements are present within all vegetable matter and are placed below in one of three groups. From these figures it is apparent that essential elements are more abundant than major elements, which in turn are present in much higher concentrations than trace elements.

   Approximate percentage of each element is by weight in dry plant matter.

ESSENTIAL ELEMENTS
Carbon (C) 44%   Oxygen (0) 44%   Hydrogen (H) 6 %

MAJOR ELEMENTS
Nitrogen (N) 1.5%   Potassium (K) 1.5%
Phosphorus (P) 0.2%   Calcium (Ca) 0.2%
Magnesium (Mg) 0.2%   Sulphur (S) 0.2%

TRACE ELEMENTS
Chlorine (Cl) 0.1%   Iron (Fe) 0.01%
Manganese (Mn) 0.01%   Zinc (Zn) 0.004%
Copper (Cu) 0.0003%   Boron (B) 0.0003%
Molybdenum (Mo) 0.00015%

Deficiencies in any of these elements show up in the developing plant. The function of each of these elements is dealt with separately and further information can be found under **Nutrients, Trace elements** and **NPK**.

Elephant manure

There is an urban myth about the vitality transmitted
to plants by elephant manure. The circus is eagerly
awaited—to collect the elephant droppings. In nutrient
and vitamin content this manure is no more valuable
than horse manure, but it has one advantage: the size
and cohesion of the pats make them easier to collect!

Enzymes

These are complex biochemical molecules which stimulate specific organic functions. Without enzymes plants could not grow, seed or reproduce; vegetable matter could not decompose, microbiological cycles would not operate and earthworms could not collect and concentrate nutrients, particularly nitrogen, phosphorus and potassium, in their casts.

Enzymes help activate photosynthesis and oxygen transfer within the plant. They speed up the fixation of nitrogen from the atmosphere but they are not part of the micro-organisms doing this work, nor are they contained in the molecular structure which uses the nitrogen. So the role of the enzyme seems elusive but it is a vital character in the plant life scenario.

Fish

The value of fish in the soil was understood long ago, when South American Incas planted their corn seed directly into a hole on top of a sardine head. Fish bones and dried fish meal have a high nutrient content, especially of phosphate. All fish material should be buried deep in the compost and covered with soil, sawdust, grass clippings or plastic sheeting; otherwise, nutritious gases will be lost and fishy smells will permeate your garden. If the temperature within your compost is high, fish remains will decompose quickly.

See also **Shellfish, Sea water** and **Seaweed**.

Fruit

Residues from juicing fruit are valuable in compost
(see **Uses and Values Table** at the back of the book).
Many people think that citrus fruits are too acid and
keep them out of the compost heap, but this is not so.
Chop the peel well for rapid decomposition.

Fruit infestations

Fruit is often spoiled by infestation of insect maggots,
such as coddling moth. Do not add infested fruit to

your compost because eggs may remain in the soil to develop into next year's population of pests. Either boil the fruit or collect it in a plastic bag, seal it and place it in the sun. Only when the maggots are dead is it safe to add it to the compost.

Fungi

Fungi are just one component in the great assembly of soil micro-organisms. They are constantly at work in the compost heap producing nutritious humus from plant residues. Fungi form networks of white threads in your compost heap and occasionally toadstools and mushrooms.

Garden waste

Any plant refuse from the garden can be composted. The rapidity of decomposition is greatly increased by chopping, mowing with a robust rotary lawn mower or by putting the waste through a muncher or shredder. See **Shredders and munchers, Grass clippings, Leaves** and **Weeds**.

Goat manure

Very similar to sheep manure in form, composition and use as a fertilizer.We have not used goat manure ourselves. It may have special attributes in addition to those of sheep manure.We do know that goat manure stimulates oil production in fruits and herbs. Visualize the goats grazing on rosemary and oregano amongst the olive groves on some steep Mediterranean shore.

Grass clippings

Grass clippings are a fantastic fuel in which to digest other plant wastes. In a pile they heat up rapidly, producing carbon dioxide, which in turn activates the process of nitrogen fixation by bacteria.

If a compost collection is developing slowly, accelerate it by adding the same volume of fresh grass clippings and covering the heap for a week or so. If you have no grass to mow for clippings, your neighbours or a mowing contractor will probably be glad to supply.

Green manures

Green manures do not just rest the soil, they revitalize it, particularly over winter. The most important function of a green manure is below the soil surface. The mass of roots stabilizes against soil erosion, aerates the soil, brings up nutrients from deep down and finally provides organic material when cut and added to the compost.

Legumes make particularly good green manures as their root nodules fix atmospheric nitrogen. They are pod bearers and include the whole range of beans, peas, clovers, lucernes, alfalfa, lupins and fenugreek. In addition to their function as green manures, most of these plants will give you a crop to enjoy.

Non-leguminous green manures include barley, rye grass, oats, millet, wheat, buckwheat, comfrey and borage. Bird seed, available from supermarkets, is also a good source of green manure. Try the one labelled Wild Bird Seed: it produces an interesting range of grains.

Harvest green manures before the plants die, leaving the roots in the ground and delivering the rest to your compost.

A range of good green manures grow from seed, available from John Chambers' Wild Flower Seeds (see **Living mulch**). Some seeds for home sprouting can be purchased from health food shops.

Guano

The dried excreta of birds and bats forms guano—phosphate-rich accumulations, built up over a long period. Probably the best guano is that from seabirds as it contains a range of trace elements present in sea water. Once deposited on limestone rocks, a mineralization process takes place. This hardens and becomes **phosphate rock**.

Many arid and tropical soils are lacking in phosphorus, and for many years guano was the only source of enrichment available. The industry was very destructive in its exploitation of phosphate rock on Pacific islands such as Nauru and Ocean Island. In Europe, cave deposits were mined.

Hair, wool and feathers

Human hair from the hairdresser's floor is a high nitrogen source as it contains one sixth of its weight in nitrogen. The same is true for animal hair, wool and bird feathers.

Hay

Hay is a compost extender and a material for mulch. The nutrient quality of the hay varies considerably. Lucerne, alfalfa and clover hays, being legumes, have a higher nitrogen content than wheaten or oaten hays.

See **Legumes** and **Nitrogen**.

Horse manure

Horses are not ruminants like cows and sheep. Feed passes through them fairly rapidly and the fresh dung is moist, not dehydrated like sheep droppings. A countryman who had a low opinion of horse manure once described it as 'all piss and straw' and indeed it is the least nutritious of the animal manures.

In spite of this, horse manure is a useful composting material, makes an excellent mulch and acts as a binder in very sandy soil. The binding property is illustrated by the fact that horse manure added to clay makes good mud bricks.

As stabled racehorses are given high protein feed some people consider this dung to be the best source of horse manure but it may contain substances toxic to soil biology (see **Contaminants and pollutants**).

Human wastes

In low rainfall areas precious fresh water is used to sweep human wastes through sewage systems and out to sea. Alternative household methods of disposal are becoming recognized by health authorities.

The Rota-Loo composts human wastes without using water. A small heater in the system evaporates fluids and a fan draws the vapour through a vent pipe to the atmosphere. The collecting tank below the toilet floor has four chambers which are rotated as each fills. The solid waste in the chambers slowly converts to an odourless humus, low in nitrogen and free of toxins. By the time the fourth chamber is in use, the first is thoroughly composted and may be removed and its contents buried in the earth.

The Biolet works on the same principle and requires little installation, only a vent pipe and a small fan heater.

Properties which process sewage and household waste water through a septic system can now discharge the fluids onto the land, as shown in the diagram. We are nourishing a young orchard in this way. All these systems, of course, require council approval.

inset

flexible hose
above ground

35 m

Septic

flexible hose attached
to standpipe

pipe 35 metres long
laid 30 metres from
house in trench
1 metre deep

overflow
Tank

submersible
pump

SEPtic
tank

Humus

Humus is a lightweight, loose, dark-coloured material which acts as a sponge to retain water and nutrients. It is the ideal end-product of composting. It will prevent soil from compacting, maintain a **pH** balance and support soil organisms, including earthworms.

A slow compost, taking a few months to mature, should contain humus. The rapid composts made in tumblers or by the Fast Fourteen recipe will not achieve the final humic stage but they will contain the elements necessary to nourish the soil and in time will form humus in the soil.

Hydrogen (H)

Hydrogen is one of the three essential elements for plant food, along with oxygen and carbon. Plants extract hydrogen from water.

Insects

Any infestation of insects in your compost heap or bin is an indication of imbalance. The presence of ants or caterpillars means the compost is too dry. Cockroaches and maggots show that their food is available and the temperature low enough for them to flourish. Heat the heap rapidly by adding grass clippings or hay.

Flies are attracted by emissions of gases, so cover compost with soil, carpet underfelt or plastic sheeting. See also **Ants, Mice, Wood lice, Slugs and snails**.

Iron (Fe)

Iron gives leaves and grasses their depth of colour. Lacking iron they tend to be yellow—anaemic, as we become when we need iron. In fact the function of iron in oxygen transfer in plants can be compared to the association of iron with haemoglobin in our bloodstream. Iron is the catalyst to carry oxygen to the leaves of plants for the synthesis of chlorophyll, the substance that gives plants their green colour.

Various iron ochres colour the soil in hues of red, brown, orange or yellow. From these iron oxides the iron is not in a form available to plants, but iron molecules from the soil can be attracted into organic compounds by the process of chelation. This process regulates iron intake and will occur naturally when there is an abundance of humus.

The chelation process can be observed where a thick mat of mulch or compost covers a red or orange clay soil but is not dug in. At first there will be a sharp line between the soil and the cover. Gradually the soil colour will lose its intensity. It will be more brown, then grey brown at the surface layer. In this way trace amounts of iron are made available for plant intake.

See **Elements** and **Chelates**.

Kitchen wastes

Kitchen wastes are often highly nitrogenous but used alone they have insufficient carbon to fuel the composting process. If the decomposition of kitchen waste is not rapid, this protein-rich material will smell bad. It will become food for pests rather than for micro-organisms which create compost. So it is essential to mix it with carbonaceous materials, such as hay, grass clippings, shredded paper and sawdust.

See also **Cooking oils and fats, Meat scraps, Fish** and **Shellfish**.

51

Leaves

Leaves of many plants and trees decompose very slowly, and they are deficient in nitrogen. So a leaf mulch used around trees and shrubs will keep weeds and grass down. It looks good but needs building up from time to time.

Leaves to be composted should be mixed with other wastes. A suitable mixture is two parts (by weight) grass clippings, three parts weeds and one part leaves. Shredding speeds up the rotting process.

Legumes

Legumes are pod-bearers. They are also nitrogen-fixing factories, gathering nitrogen by means of bacteria in root nodules. In addition, the deep roots of legumes bring up nutrients, including trace elements, from the sub-soil.

They provide us with bean and pea seeds to eat; flowers for the house, such as lupins and sweet peas; and fodder for stock, including clover, alfalfa and lucerne hay. All these plants are valuable in compost.

See also **Clover, Green manure, Hay, Living mulch** and **Nitrogen**.

Liming

Lime is applied to reduce soil acidity. It sweetens the soil, introduces valuable nutrients and conditions the soil for proper water percolation.

One form of lime is ground limestone (calcium carbonate) but the best is ground dolomite (magnesium calcium carbonate). Following dolomite application, weak acids in the soil release carbon dioxide from the rock flour, leaving behind the alkaline hydroxides of calcium and magnesium. This natural chemical reaction works on a large scale over a long time span to form caves in limestone country.

Limestone or dolomite can be applied directly to soil at the time of planting seedlings or sowing seed. It is best to add them to compost at the end of the composting process as they may otherwise adversely affect the bacterial cycles.

Another form, slaked lime (hydrate of calcium), must be applied two weeks before planting seedlings or sowing seed and should not be added to compost while it is working. It is not a natural product and can damage the roots of plants.

Wood ash also acts as a liming substance.

Liming is hardly necessary in most of the British Isles, but it is essential in porous quartz, sandy soils which may be present in estuarine conditions.

The beneficial nutrients from liming are discussed with **Dolomite** and **Wood ash**.

Liquid manures and teas

In small gardens where it may be impractical to make compost, liquid manures and teas are invaluable. Comfrey alone contains so many nutrients that, as a tea, it may keep a garden in good health without any animal manure at all.

Animal manures, seaweed, comfrey leaves, dandelions, stinging nettles, yarrow and molasses are all very beneficial. To make a tea, lay the substance in a closed container and cover with plenty of rainwater. Stir every day or so. After three weeks it should be ready to use. Concentrated worm-cast liquid manure is available commercially, under names such as 'Worm Drops'.

Liquid manures and teas may be applied, diluted, directly to plants or added to the compost as **accelerators**.

Living mulch

Living mulches are plants that feed us and the soil. Many legumes can be grown for this purpose, such as broad beans, cow peas, alfalfa and red and white clovers. These crops provide mulch and edible seed and sprouts, and their root nodules fix nitrogen . Non-legumes which benefit both the soil and us include buckwheat and millet.

New Zealand spinach is a natural seashore stabilizer and has succulent leaves which mulch readily and provide an excellent substitute for spinach.

Sources for seeds of the above plants include John Chambers' Wild Flower Seeds (15 Westleigh Road, Barton Seagrave, Kettering, Northants NN15 5AJ, phone 0933 652562), Chiltern Seeds (Bortree Stile, Ulverston, Cumbria LA12 7PB, phone 0229 581137) and Sutton Seeds Ltd (Hele Road, Torquay, Devon TQ2 7QJ, phone 0803 614455).

A mulching technique is discussed under the **Clover** entry.

Magnesium (Mg)

Magnesium is critical for plant development. Without it there would be no green plants. Magnesium is one of the catalysts in the production of chlorophyll, the substance that greens leaves. It also assists in water regulation, absorption of nitrogen, phosphorus and sulphur and helps in the formation of proteins and other biochemical complexes.

Ground dolomite rock rectifies a magnesium deficiency. It also provides supplementary calcium and is a liming substance, adjusting acidity in the soil.

Manganese (Mn)

This element is involved in the photosynthetic process. Though present in most soils, it has to be converted into soluble **chelate** salts so that it is available to plants. This is achieved by microbiological activity. Seaweed, lucerne or other legume hays will contribute ample manganese to a diverse compost mixture.

Manures

See **Animal manures**.

Meat scraps

Provided your compost is working and the temperature in the centre is high, you can add meat scraps to it. Make a hole in the centre and put the scraps in, then cover with a handful of sawdust or grass clippings. The heat should 'cook' any maggots and the cover will protect the compost from flies, etc.

Mice

If mice burrow or make nests in your compost, it shows that protein foods are not being broken down. The heap needs to be revitalized with the addition of heat-producing materials, such as grass clippings. A dramatic increase in temperature will persuade the mice to move. A cat would remove the mice but it can't assist in maturing the compost. Pests are an indicator that all is not well with the digesting process in the heap.

Micro-organisms

These include algae, bacteria, fungi, protozoa and yeasts. Simplistic in form yet complex in their biochemical interactions, they form a microcosm within the soil. Their life and work creates and maintains soil in a way that sustains plants.

Micro-organisms assist in making elements acceptable for plant intake. They concentrate minerals and link them with organic compounds to form **chelates**. The chelating process is so powerful that it can corrode rock into soil.

Temperature, moisture, aeration, and pH dictate microbiological activity in the soil. When conditions are just right for a particular group of organisms, its population will develop explosively. For example, when compost is tossed and aired the anaerobic bacteria that flourish in a closed heap will be almost instantaneously replaced by an aerobic population.

Approximate quantity of micro-organisms to each gram of soil:

algae	100,000
bacteria	1,000,000,000
fungi	1,000,000
protozoa	1,000,000
yeasts	1,000

Molasses

A residue from the process of refining cane sugar, molasses is a wonderful **chelator**.

Mix one cup of molasses in 10 litres of warm rainwater and sprinkle onto the accumulated compost. Cover it up or your heap may be visited by a swarm of bees. The resulting acceleration of the fermentation process is exciting—measure it daily with a thermometer.

Molasses can be obtained cheaply from bulk health food stores; take your own container.

Molybdenum (Mo)

Of all the trace elements molybdenum is absorbed by plants in the most minute amounts, yet it is a vital element, a catalyst in the bacterial activity of fixing atmospheric nitrogen.

The leguminous hays, alfalfa, clover and lucerne contain enriched concentrations of moly. Seaweeds also have significant quantities.

The minute dose of moly required by plants can be satisfied by a balanced compost, both in terms of constituents and the acidity-alkalinity scale (see **pH**).

A deficiency of this element is probably due to an acid soil and can be rectified by liming.

Mulch

Grass clippings, hay or straw can be used, also newspaper and cardboard, pinned down by weights. These materials will eventually join the soil but as mulches they are nutrient deficient. As they are totally aerated, developing gases escape and there is no anaerobic phase to concentrate nutrients.

You can spread mulch around young plants that are developing well and some seedlings can be planted directly into mulch, provided they have enough soil surrounding their roots. Potatoes thrive in deep mulch. As their roots grow sideways rather than downwards, mulch can be added as the plant grows. In this way the greening of potatoes is prevented. Potatoes exposed to the sun develop the greening substance, solanine, to which many people are allergic.

Carpet underfelt can be used as a water- and nutrient-retaining mulch for vegetable growing in arid sandy soils, such as coastal sand dunes.

For more on mulches, see **Living mulch** and **Clover**.

Nitrogen (N)

Nitrogen stimulates leaf growth as well as helping to feed the plant. It ensures seed fertility and reproductive fidelity through genetic imprinting.

Nitrogen is a vital plant nutrient. It is the linchpin in many biochemical molecules, including all proteins, amino acids, chlorophyll and the DNA molecules.

Gaseous nitrogen occupies four-fifths of Earth's atmosphere, yet it cannot be absorbed directly into cells or tissue. It can only be absorbed when 'fixed' in

Nitrogen-fixing Nodules

combination with other elements. Some of this fixation occurs due to electrical storms, but mostly it is through microbiological activity in the decomposition of natural materials.

Nitrogen can combine with hydrogen to form gaseous ammonia and in the composting process this gas should be confined to the inside of the heap. If you get the smells associated with fresh manures, cover the heap with more material or soil—you are wasting a product that will later become a valuable nitrate.

Nitrogen can combine with other nutrients, say potassium and oxygen to form potassium nitrate. Such nitrates are readily soluble and can be absorbed by plants.

Legumes fix large amounts of nitrogen from the atmosphere by root bacteria contained in root nodules, often visible to the naked eye (see **Legumes,** also **Green manures** and **Clover**). Experiments on this phenomenon in the United States found that over a ten-year period nitrogen fixed by alfalfa = 281 kg per hectare, red clover = 188 kg per hectare, soya beans = 118 kg per hectare and field peas = 54 kg per hectare.

NPK

This refers to the chemical abbreviations for nitrogen— N, phosphorus—P and potassium—K, which are the major plant nutrients. Nitrogen stimulates leaf growth. Phosphorus enhances seed and fruit formation. Potassium strengthens stems, increases root growth and helps in the setting of fruit.

The proportions of NPK in artificial fertilizers vary according to the application. For example, a rose fertilizer has an NPK balance differing from a citrus or lawn food. Such precision cannot be achieved with organic fertilizers. A properly developed compost, however, is a complete plant food. If such composts are applied to a garden regularly, plant problems of all kinds should diminish.

Nutrients

Plants absorb nutrients from the air and from the soil. With these nutrients they make a complexity of organic molecules, which in specific combinations enable plants to flourish. These include glucose, cellulose, proteins, essential oils, amino acids, vitamins and chlorophyll—all substances vital for plant growth and reproduction.

The essential **elements**—carbon, oxygen and hydrogen—are absorbed by plants as gaseous vapours. The other thirteen elements are transmitted to the plant from the soil, compost, mulch or manure. While mulches are usually nutrient deficient, they do hold moisture which is essential to the process of nutrient intake by plants.

Any soil, however nutrient rich it may be, needs to be revitalized as plants constantly draw nutrients from it. Composts and manures bear the raw materials from which nutrients are derived, so apply them regularly and you will get striking results from your garden.

Oxygen (O)

One of the three essential elements present in all vegetable matter. Plants absorb oxygen both directly from the atmosphere and through chemical reactions involving water or water vapour. See also **Elements**.

Paper

This is an excellent compost extender; it works best if applied torn up. Wetted paper also makes a good mulch if weighted down. Paper mulching retains moisture and multiplies earthworm activity around trees.

Please note: newsprint ink no longer contains harmful substances, such as metallic lead and cadmium. Although newspaper, computer and other office papers are benign to plants and soil organisms, the coated papers of coloured magazines are suspect. See also **Cardboard** and **Cartons**.

pH

Traditionally, soil that tasted sour or bitter was regarded as unsuitable for growing crops. Sour soils were too acid and bitter soils too alkaline. A sweet-tasting soil was known to be fertile.

Today we measure soil acidity and alkalinity in

terms of pH units, pH standing for the power of hydrogen and the relationship between hydrogen ions (H+) and hydroxyl ions (OH-). The more hydrogen ions the greater the acidity, whilst hydroxyl ions dominate in alkaline environments.

The pH scale ranges from 1—extremely acid, to 14—extremely alkaline. A balance is achieved at 7, which is termed neutral. The optimum pH for the majority of common plants is between 6, 5 and 7. At this level soils will support the full range of microbiological activity favourable for healthy plant growth.

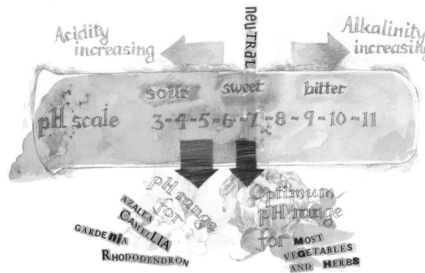

Note that the pH range for the ornamental shrubs is not compatible with that for the more common vegetables.

pH testers are commercially available and you may find them advertised in garden magazines or at your local garden centre.

Phosphate rock

Phosphate rock is barely soluble in water but, if the rock is ground to a powder, organic humic acids in the soil will release phosphorus. This powdered phosphate rock contains a range of trace elements from the diet of seabirds. It is a terrific compost supplement. Details regarding availability and application can be obtained from the Henry Doubleday Research Association, Convent Lane, Bocking, Braintree, Essex.

Phosphorus (P)

Phosphorus is a vital element in all biological energy transfer systems, such as the conversion of solar energy into chemical energy with the formation of chlorophyll and glucose. It encourages fruit development and fertility of the resultant seed.

Bones and other skeletal material, such as prawn shells, are rich in phosphorus. Other phosphorus sources are from accumulations of animal manure, seabirds in particular but also bats. Earthworm casts are also rich in phosphorus.

See **Blood and bone, Shellfish, Phosphate rock** and **Guano**.

Photosynthesis

Plants, algae and certain bacteria are distinguished from all other organisms by the biochemical process called photosynthesis. It is a complexity of reactions which convert solar energy into chemical energy in the presence of carbon dioxide and water for the manufacture of cell materials. The carbon dioxide is generated by the decaying of vegetation in the composting process.

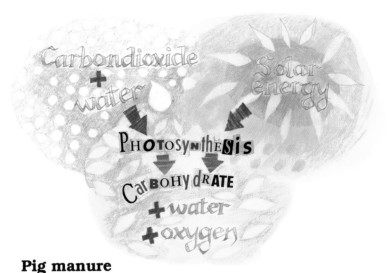

Carbondioxide
+
water

Solar energy

PHOTOSYNTHESIS

Carbohydrate
+ water
+ oxygen

Pig manure

Pig manure is reputed to strengthen root development and is particularly good for potatoes, sweet potatoes and other tuber crops. It must be well composted.

Pigeon manure

This is the richest form of manure produced by domestic animals. Use as for **chicken manure**. If you can only collect a small amount, put it in a container with rain-water, cover and leave for three weeks. Dilute the mixture and use as a **liquid manure**.

Plastics

Plastics are not biodegradable but thick plastic sheeting is excellent for covering the compost heap. It keeps the flies out, holds moisture and odours in, and prevents nutrients escaping in the form of gases. In

heavy rain an uncovered heap becomes soggy and
bacterial action is set back.

Plastic bags make good containers in which to
render **weeds** and even **fruit infestations** harmless.
Seal tightly and leave in the sun until contents have
decomposed.

Potassium (K)

Potassium is a major plant nutrient in the form of
potash (K_2O). Although it does not occur within plant-
forming molecules, it is involved in complex
biochemical interactions, such as starch, sugar and
protein formation, and in photosynthesis. It increases
root growth, strengthens stems and assists in setting
fruit and brilliance of flower colour.

Potassium is contained in most organic materials,
although some, such as **wood ash, soot and seaweed**,
are richer than others. Other potassium-rich minerals
are granite and basalt **rock flours**, so if your soil is of
granite or basalt origin, you will not have a potash
deficiency.

Commercial fertilizers usually contain potassium
chloride. Such potash salts are so readily soluble that
they may cause the plant to absorb excess potash
which can inhibit assimilation of other nutrients, such
as phosphorus. This problem does not occur in organic
sources as the intake of nutrients by the plant is both
slower and more balanced.

Potting and seedling mix

Mix three parts well-matured compost with one part
fine, washed sand. Cover seeds with sieved compost,
not sand. Charcoal can be used for drainage; it also
absorbs nutrients which are released again through
watering. If you are concerned about harmful organisms
in your mixture, put it in the deep freeze for a few days.

Plastic sheeting over compost HEAP

Recipes

Fast Fourteen

David devised this special recipe as a quick-fix compost. It is reliable, nutritious and works every time. It is dependent on careful preparation of materials, but does not necessarily require special equipment.

Quantities are expressed in 10-litre buckets and will give a large heap. The quantities can be reduced, but not increased.

4 buckets fresh grass clippings
8 buckets garden waste, chopped with a spade
8 buckets lucerne, hay or chaff (chopped hay)
2 buckets bran
2-4 buckets animal manure (depending on freshness
and quality—2 buckets of chicken manure is ample but
4 buckets of horse manure is not enough)
2 cups molasses mixed with 1/4 cup seaweed extract
in 2 buckets of warm rainwater

Fast Fourteen Compost – covered heap – Murray Valley – Spring

Showing anaerobic phase followed by aerobic phase after tossing.

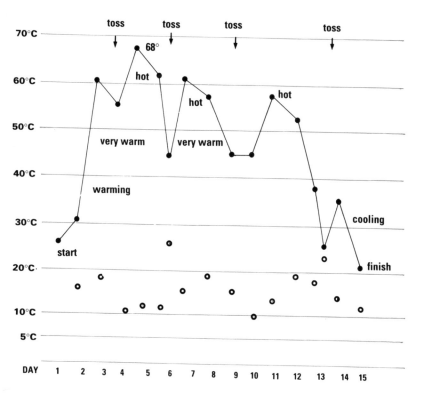

- ● temperature inside compost heap
- ○ outside air temperature

Bran and molasses are available from health food stores and lucerne, hay, chaff and animal manure may sometimes be obtained from produce merchants.

Mix all ingredients together well. If in a heap, cover with a plastic sheet. It will take two to four days for the mixture to heat up. Add water if dry; keep moist but not saturated. Toss and turn every third day thereafter until compost cools to air temperature. Mix in 1 handful of dolomite and 2 handfuls of wood ash. The compost is now ready. It will cover a good 2 to 3 square metres of soil.

Depending on what materials you have available, any of the following recipes will make adequate compost. You may find it useful to refer to **Temperature** and the **Uses and Values Table** on the inside front cover. Nutrient content increases from recipe 1 through to 4; however, Fast Fourteen is the most complete.

Recipe 1. 12 parts grass clippings, 1 part sawdust

Recipe 2. 2 parts grass clippings, 3 parts weeds, 1 part leaves

Recipe 3. 2 parts weeds, 3 parts paper, 2 parts lucerne, hay or chaff

Recipe 4. 3 parts weeds, 3 parts leaves, 1 part paper, 1 part chicken litter, 1 part (by volume) of diluted seaweed solution

After mixing the ingredients for any of these recipes, proceed as for Fast Fourteen.

Rock flours and dusts

Granite and basalt rocks have a high potassium content and may contain significant traces of calcium, magnesium and phosphorus, depending on their origin. They are an excellent compost supplement if applied in a powdered form. A monumental mason might be prepared to supply you, or contact the Henry Doubleday Research Association (see **Phosphate rock**).

For comments on rock nutrients see **Potassium,
Phosphate rock** and **Dolomite**.

Sawdust

Saw-mills and joineries produce a lot of sawdust. It is
mainly composed of cellulose and has a high
carbon/low nitrogen content (see **The Carbon/Nitrogen
Cone** at the back of the book). To compensate, compost
sawdust with highly nitrogenous materials such as fruit
and vegetable wastes, animal manure and/or seaweed.

A bulk quantity of sawdust is very useful but
don't compost it all at once. Keep it in a heap, well
watered, for at least a month. It can then be added to
your compost a bit at a time. Sawdust can also be
used as a mulch.

Sea water

Despite its high salinity, sea water is very nutritious. It
is constantly replenished with chemicals from coastal
runoff and deep sea volcanism along fracture zones
and so it contains a complete range of both major and
minor elements needed for plant growth.

Some people add sea water to compost; say one
part sea water to a hundred parts rainwater.
Asparagus, kale, New Zealand spinach, beetroot and
silverbeet all originated on sea sprayed shorelines.
They may benefit from spraying in the same
proportions as your compost.

The best way to utilize sea water chemistry is to
use **seaweed**—raw, dried or as a liquid extract.

Seaweed

Seaweed is the perfect compost additive as all the
necessary nutrients are concentrated in it from sea
water.

Figures cited over page show seaweed is highly

enriched in nutrients. Seaweed absorbs these elements as separate entities (ions), not as combinations (compounds). So sea salt (sodium chloride) is not concentrated or even present, in that form, in seaweed. Thus seaweed is not harmful as an additive to soil or compost. From the figures below you can see the high enrichment it contains.

Collect seaweed as fresh as possible because it loses its nutrients rapidly, particularly nitrogen. No need to wash, just chop with a spade and spread as a mulch or add into compost. Alternatively make a liquid tea. If you are using seaweed as your major nutrient and trace element source, add dolomite to the soil when applying compost to your garden beds as seaweed does not concentrate magnesium.

Element	Concentration in sea water (mg/1)	Seaweed enrichment factor relative to sea water
Carbon	20.8	x 12,300
Nitrogen	0.5	x 8,000
Phosphorus	0.07	x 50,000
Potassium	380.00	x 140
Calcium	400.00	x 750
Magnesium	1350.00	x 4
Sulphur	885.00	x 14
Iron	0.01	x 70,000
Manganese	0.002	x 26,500
Zinc	0.01	x 15,000
Boron	4.60	x 24
Copper	0.003	x 2,300
Molybdenum	0.01	x 45
Iodine	0.06	x 500 to 25,000

Seaweed extract

These concentrates, usually of bull kelp, are excellent. The commercial products seem expensive but they go a long way: 10 ml diluted in 1 litre of rainwater acts as a foliage spray for fruit trees and makes a highly nutritious additive to a household compost bin.

A dried meal from seaweed is also available commercially.

Sheep manure

Sheep, like cows, are ruminants, but the manure differs considerably. Sheep manure is dropped as pellets and is dehydrated. It is a concentrated product with a relatively high potassium content. Various biochemical compounds are also concentrated, including amino acids and enzymes.

These compounds increase the aroma of fruit and flowers and the oil content of herbs. When sheep are grazed on mint the oil content of the mint is increased . . . intriguing, as we eat roast lamb with mint sauce or jelly.

Sheep manure is an accumulating problem under a shearing shed. To the gardener who can collect the manure it is a great gift. Spread generously over established beds or on spoiled hay for immediate planting or sowing of seed.

Outstanding results can be obtained from sheep manure. Most striking are sweet peas with bright, strong colours, good perfume and thick flower stalks up to 50 cm long. This reflects the potassium content, since potassium reinforces stalk and stem fibres and enhances flowering. Sheep manure also strengthens root development.

Sheep manure enriches compost, but add it at the end of the composting process, with dolomite and/or wood ash.

Shellfish

Shellfish are a diverse group of marine animals whose soft parts are edible and whose hard parts, their shells, are rich in plant foods. Prawn, lobster and crayfish shells are composed of chitin, as are our fingernails, and bonded together with nitrogen, phosphorus and calcium. Bury them deep in your working compost heap and soon they and their smells will dissolve into plant food.

Oyster and mussel shells are basically calcium carbonate, with varying amounts of nitrogen, phosphorus, potassium and trace elements. Mussel shells disintegrate quicker than do oyster shells, which should be broken up before adding to compost.

Shredders and munchers

The small, electric-powered 'munchers' will reduce kitchen and garden wastes to piles of finely chopped material which will compost more rapidly than bulk waste. Shredders are larger, petrol-driven machines. They take thicker material, are faster and more robust. A good rotary lawn mower can chop up compost materials that are not too soggy.

In small gardens no machinery is needed. Most materials can be chopped with a sharpened garden spade.

Slaters

Slaters are land-living relatives of crabs and lobsters. Also known as wood lice or pill bugs, they are unjustly labelled as pests since they do no harm to plants. Their part in the decomposition of vegetable matter is in working over yeasts and fungi. If they are browsing over your compost the moisture content will be just right.

Slugs and snails

Although much loathed for their destructive work in the garden, slugs and snails do have a function in the composting process. Their rows of teeth, called radulae, and their mucous membranes digest cellulose, including newspaper and cardboard.

The leopard slug, which is much larger than the usual garden slug and easily recognizable, is of particular help in a heap of well wilted material. It eats

only dead vegetation and plant products such as paper.

Some breeds of ducks eat slugs and snails, ferreting them out with great gusto.

If you have to kill snails, their shells add calcium and other minerals to the heap.

Stinging nettles

Stinging nettles contain iron for green leaf production and are high in nitrogen. Add leaves to the compost as an **accelerator** or make **liquid manure** for green leaf plantings.

Strip trenching

This system of rejuvenating established garden beds makes compost and manure go a long way. With a narrow hoe make trenches 10 cm wide and deep with a 10-cm space between rows. In the first and third trenches place fresh or mature manure; in the second trench, compost. Sow seed or transplant seedlings into the compost trench and compact the soil well. As the plants develop, their roots will benefit from the trenches of manure. The next crop is planted into the manured trenches. Worms will be very active in these trenches.

plant first crop IN COMPOST

Trench 1   2   3

plant second crop IN MANURE

materials are well-blended by crop No 2

Sulphur (S)

Sulphur is present in all plant materials and in all but
very sandy soils. In a decomposing covered compost
heap it becomes concentrated by sulphur-forming
bacteria. Disturb the heap and smell the rotten egg
gas— hydrogen sulphide.

   With aeration, in warmed soil or compost, free
sulphur or sulphides will oxidize and combine with
other elements. They form sulphate salts of iron,
potassium, calcium, magnesium and so on. These
sulphates are soluble in water so the plants can
absorb them. The sulphides, such as the mineral
pyrite (iron sulphide), are insoluble in water. No matter

how much pyrite is available, plants cannot absorb it.

Sulphur is important within proteins, enzymes and vitamins. Composts which have digested kitchen and garden wastes will have the correct balance of sulphur. Leaves of the cabbage family are particularly rich in sulphur— think of the smell of boiling cabbage.

Soils are seldom deficient in sulphur but in industrial areas it can be a pollutant, inhibiting plant growth. Acid rain in North America and Europe is also caused by sulphur emitted as an industrial waste product to the air.

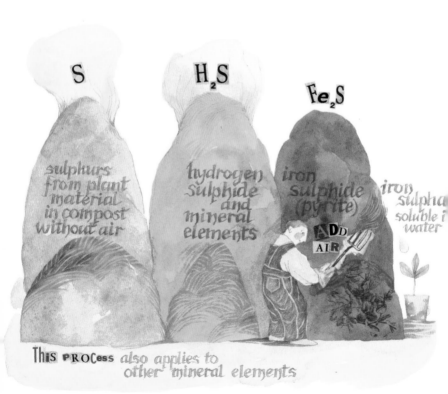

S

sulphurs from plant material in compost without air

H_2S

hydrogen sulphide and mineral elements

Fe_2S

iron sulphide (pyrite)

ADD AIR

iron sulpha soluble i water

This PROCess also applies to other mineral elements

Superphosphate

Superphosphate and triple superphosphate are manufactured by treating phosphate rock with sulphuric acid. Phosphoric acid, a more soluble form of phosphate, is released.

Super has an abundance of sulphur which causes a microbiological imbalance in the soil. The production of humus in the soil is therefore reduced and acidity increased. All that Super leaves in the soil is a residue of harmful salts which discourages earthworms. When the microbiological life around them in the soil is not destroyed, earthworms concentrate organic phosphate. So, not only does Super impair the quality of your soil ultimately but it also inhibits the natural processes for concentrating phosphate. Further, the manufacture of superphosphate and the synthetic nitrogenous fertilizers involves high energy-consuming industries.

Tea leaves

Empty the teapot into compost or mulch. It has a high nitrogen content and also contains phosphorus and potash.

Temperature

Compost needs cooking. The graphs on pages 67 and 79 show changes in temperature during the cooking process in both covered heaps and tumblers. Increased temperatures are generated by anaerobic bacteria when air is excluded. By tossing or turning, aeration occurs and temperature drops, building up again as air is excluded. A gradual cooling is apparent until a constant temperature is reached which approximates that of the air outside. You can feel the temperature fluctuations by thrusting your hand deep into the compost. You won't keep it there for long if the temperature is above 60°C. The high temperatures help to purify the finished product by cooking weed seed, eggs and larvae of insects and nematode worms, as well as chemically changing organic toxins into harmless substances.

If you want to be more precise or set a project for high school students, use a thermometer rather than your hand. We use a preserving thermometer after having ruined two normal air thermometers in heated compost. If you want to demonstrate the power of a hot compost heap, wrap a raw egg in aluminium foil and place it in the middle of the heap. Come back in a couple of hours to a hard-boiled egg.

Trace elements

In minute quantities these elements are essential in many plant functions. Chlorine, iron, manganese, zinc, molybdenum, copper and boron are micro-nutrients, often acting as catalysts rather than being part of a complex molecule. Deficiencies are reflected in plant growth abnormalities: whip tail in cauliflower is caused by molybdenum deficiency, yellow citrus leaves lack iron.

A trace element which is present in the soil in larger amounts than is required is a pollutant. High concentrations of any trace element will be toxic to some plants. Each species of plant has its own requirements and tolerances. Compost, which includes a variety of materials such as legume hays, animal manures and/or seaweed, will contain a balanced mix of trace elements.

Dramatic changes of vegetation are a useful tool in mineral exploration. On aerial photographs or satellite imagery, where plant growth has been adversely affected in an area of country, a rich deposit of minerals such as copper may be seen.

Tumblers

We have had great success with our home-made tumbler. It is a quick and efficient way to make compost. Make sure you have a good carbon/nitrogen mixture (see **The Carbon/Nitrogen Cone** at the back of the book). Chop or shred the waste materials. Fill the tumbler to about three quarters capacity. If the mixture is too dry, add water. Rotate the tumbler once or twice a day. Compost should be ready in ten days.

Here we have given a graph to illustrate how we made a quick compost in our tumbler over nine days. This was in mid-winter in Sydney, Australia, where several of the mornings were relatively cold. The tumbler was turned twice a day. Just before turning the temperature inside the mixture was recorded, as was the air temperature. The materials were a general mixture, shredded, and the only accelerator was grass clippings.

This tumbler was made from a forty-four gallon drum and the heating of the metal drum probably helped to get the compost started in mid-winter. Commercial tumblers are also available.

See also **Temperature**.

tumble tumble tumble

twice a day

Water

Plants have a liquid rather than a solid diet, so nutrients need to be dissolved in water for rapid absorption. Two of the major plant nutrients, oxygen and hydrogen, are combined as H_2O to form water, so water is an essential component for plant growth and nutrition.

Compost must be kept moist for it to be biologically activated and nutrients transmitted. Remember green plant material in a compost provides quite a lot of moisture, so don't over-water or you will have a soggy, slow-maturing, smelly mess, dominated by **anaerobic bacteria**. If this happens, add dry material such as straw or sawdust.

Another consideration is **water purity**, discussed below.

Water purity

Water is a troublesome question because its chemistry can affect microbiological activity and thus the maturation of the compost. Consider the quality of available water, whether it be out of a tap, from the sky, out of the ground or from a river. Reticulated town water supplies are often chlorinated and contaminated with organic substances. In such circumstances weak organic chlorides and sulphides may be produced which effect the micro-environment.

Rainwater can be acid and may absorb heavy metals such as lead, so in much of Western Europe the collection of rainwater cannot be recommended because it can affect the micro-biological balance of the compost as well as contaminating it with complex molecules bonded with metals.

River water flowing through settled farming areas may be even more deleterious to compost-making with the infiltration of residues from herbicides, insecticides and fungicides. The addition of artificial fertilizers alters the chemical balance and increases salinity.

Bore water should be analysed before using it on compost as it may contain a high level of minerals or dissolved salts and an unacceptable **pH** level. A good point about underground water is that undesirable organic molecules are usually absent. This water has undergone natural filtration before entering the aquifer strata which has been tapped by the bore.

Town or river water can be neutralized in modern filter systems if it is suspected that water is affecting your compost.

Weather

Warm or hot weather will help a fresh heap of material to begin the complex biochemical processes which create compost but hot or cold weather is not a very significant factor. If a collection of suitable ingredients is put together in a heap, the cooking and digesting will begin. In cold periods the process will be retarded but not stopped. A cover in cold weather helps the initial warming that is necessary. In wet weather it will protect the heap from too much rain.

Weeds

Weeds are plants growing in the wrong place. Some were introduced as ornamental plants and others grow from seed contaminating commercial seed or in bird or other animal droppings.

Weeds from the garden can be composted—get them before they seed. The following must be treated separately: nut grass, onion weed, oxalis and *Tradescantia*, known as wandering jew or creeping gentile. Dig these up carefully with all their roots and corms, pack them into opaque plastic bags with a little water and seal tightly. Keep in a warm spot for some months, until they have rotted completely.

Hay, straw and free-range animal manures may contain a variety of weed seed which will germinate if not burnt up in the composting process. If manure is applied directly to beds, burying it or covering it with mulch will reduce the weed problem. Learn to identify weeds in their early growth when they are easy to remove. **Stinging nettles** often grow out of free-range manure—cherish them as a compost additive for their iron and calcium content.

Wine

Residues and pressings from the wine making process make good compostable material and are especially high in potassium.

Wood ash and soot

Wood ash is a valuable source of potash (K_2O). When it is derived from eucalypt hardwoods it also contains useful amounts of phosphate and an array of trace elements. The soot from wood fires concentrates these nutrients in even greater amounts.

Fresh ash is very alkaline and can upset the **pH** balance of your compost, so add at maturation, as for lime and dolomite. The alkalinity could also burn young plant roots, so when applying to seed beds spread ash 10 cm from rows of seedlings.

Coal ash is suspect and should not be used, due to high tar and sulphur content.

Wood lice see Slaters

Worms

The term is fairly meaningless as there are many worm-like creatures which are totally unrelated to each other. Those which inhabit soil and rotting vegetation include:

The annelids—the most important group, see **Earthworms**.

The platyhelminthes—flat, arrow-headed, slimy worms that travel by expanding and contracting like elastic. They live under rocks as well as in rotting vegetation. It is not unusual to find them on the edge of a compost heap and although they look and feel repulsive, they may be useful; their slime or mucous may play a part in decomposing vegetation.

The nematodes—round, thread-like worms, including eelworms. Many of these are harmful to plants, being parasitic within the plant roots. Soil nematodes can be controlled by mulching thickly with compost. This organic matter contains fungi which entrap and destroy nematodes: an example of simple biological control of pests by organic means.

yarrow
tea

Yarrow

Yarrow belongs to a group of herbs of the genus *Achillea*—mythologically powerful in healing Achilles' heel but also biochemically powerful in compost. Yarrow contains a complexity of organic compounds to stimulate microbiological activity and makes a potent liquid tea to accelerate compost activity.

Yeasts

Yeasts are significant in the fermentation process of composting. Although present in rotting vegetation, particularly fruit, the process can be accelerated by adding brewer's or baker's yeast, bread scraps, Marmite, yoghurt or buttermilk.

Yoghurt and buttermilk

Yoghurt and buttermilk ferment readily and produce yeasts and other micro-organisms. Leftovers added to the compost heap will act as **accelerators**.

Zinc (Zn)

Although present in plants in minute traces, zinc is an essential component of several plant enzymes. These enzymes are involved in the formation of complex organic compounds and in the regulation of water.

Adequate zinc is provided by seaweed, corn stalks and all animal manures.

The Carbon/Nitrogen Compost Diet Cone

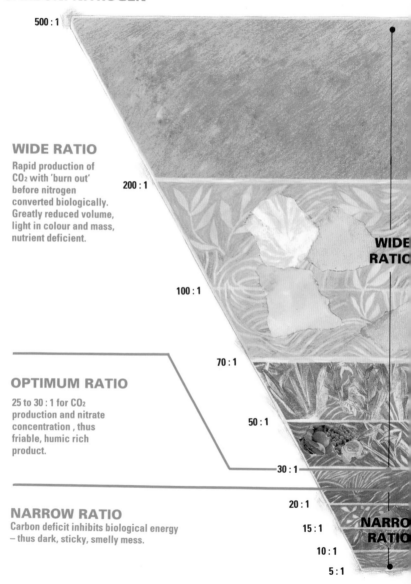

CARBON: NITROGEN

500 : 1

WIDE RATIO

Rapid production of CO_2 with 'burn out' before nitrogen converted biologically. Greatly reduced volume, light in colour and mass, nutrient deficient.

200 : 1

100 : 1

WIDE RATIO

70 : 1

OPTIMUM RATIO

25 to 30 : 1 for CO_2 production and nitrate concentration , thus friable, humic rich product.

50 : 1

30 : 1

20 : 1

NARROW RATIO

Carbon deficit inhibits biological energy – thus dark, sticky, smelly mess.

15 : 1

NARROW RATIO

10 : 1

5 : 1

This diagram shows that a varied diet is necessary to achieve best results, optimum ratio being between 25 and 30 to 1.

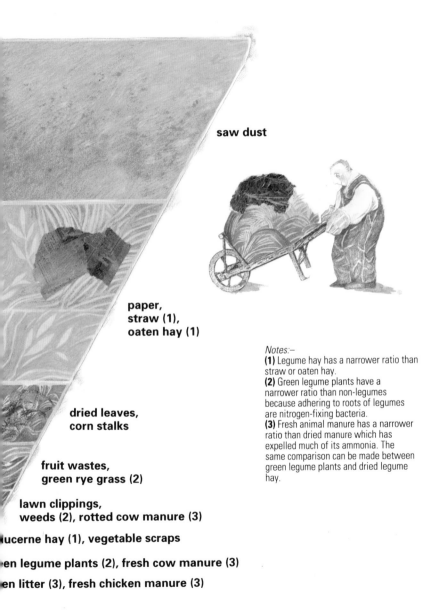

saw dust

paper,
straw (1),
oaten hay (1)

dried leaves,
corn stalks

fruit wastes,
green rye grass (2)

lawn clippings,
weeds (2), rotted cow manure (3)

lucerne hay (1), vegetable scraps

green legume plants (2), fresh cow manure (3)

chicken litter (3), fresh chicken manure (3)

Notes:–
(1) Legume hay has a narrower ratio than straw or oaten hay.
(2) Green legume plants have a narrower ratio than non-legumes because adhering to roots of legumes are nitrogen-fixing bacteria.
(3) Fresh animal manure has a narrower ratio than dried manure which has expelled much of its ammonia. The same comparison can be made between green legume plants and dried legume hay.

Uses and Values of Composting Materials

COMPOSTING MATERIALS

COMPOSTING MATERIALS	MULCH/FILLER	ACCELERATOR	ADDITIVES	N	P	K	Ca	Mg	S	Cl	Fe	Mn	Zn	Cu	B	Mo
Banana stalks				○	■											
Blood & bone		✓		■	●	●	+	+	+		+					
Bran	✓			●	●	●		+	+							
Cardboard	✓✓															
Carpet underfelt	✓✓															
Chicken manure – fresh *		✓		●	○		+	+	+	+		+		+	+	
Clever Clover	✓	✓		●	●		+	+	+	+						
Comfrey		✓	✓	●	●	●	+	+	+	+	+	+	+	+	+	
Cow manure – fresh *		✓	✓	○	○		■	+	+	○			+	+		
Dandelions			✓	●	●		+	+		+			+	+		?
Dolomite			✓			■	+	+		+		+	+	+	+	?
Duck manure – fresh *		✓	✓	●	○	+	+	+	+	+	?	+		+	+	
Earthworm cast		✓	✓	●	●	+	+	+	+	+	+	?	?	?	?	
Egg shells			✓	●	+	+	+	+								
Feathers				■												
Fish meal		✓	✓	□	●	+	+	+	+	+	+	+	+	+	+	
Fungi	✓✓			□												
Goat manure		✓	✓	●	○	+	+	+	+	+	+					
Grass clippings	✓✓	✓		●	+	+	+	+	+	+	+					
Green manure – legumes	✓	✓		■	+	+	+	+	+	+				+		
– non-legumes	✓			○	○					+						
Guano – bat				+	●	+	+	+		+		+				
Hair				■												
Hay – legume	✓✓			●	●		+	+		+				+		
– non-legume	✓✓			○	○											
Horse & Elephant manure *	✓	✓		○	○											

Limestone

Micro-organisms – aerobic

– anaerobic

Molasses

Paper

Phosphate rock

Pigeon manure – fresh *

Pig manure – fresh *

Prawn shells

Rabbit manure *

Rock flour – granitic and basaltic

Sawdust

Sea water

Sea weed – fresh *

– meal

– liquid extract

Self mulching legumes

N.Z. Spinach

Sheep manure – fresh *

Slugs & Snails – living

– shells

Stinging nettles

Wastes – Citrus

– Coffee

– Garden

– Kitchen

– Wine pressings

Wood ash (*Eucalyptus*)

Yarrow

Yeasts and Yoghurt

* Dried manure contains less nitrogen
and micro-organism activity

✓ Important

■ more than 10%
□ 5 – 10%
● 1 – 5%
○ 0 – 1%
+ trace
? possible trace

elemental content as percentage of dry matter.

Your compost record

Here is an example of how to record your compost making activities.

Method: **Tumbler**
       Heap
       Bin

Date Started : 3 /July / 92
Date Finished : 11 / " "
Date Used : 13 / " "

Location *Glovers garden*

Where and how applied:

Composition:

Old garden strip trench

4 Buckets lawn clippings. 5 Buckets green garden was
2 Buckets mature chicken manure. 2 Buckets chopped
dry grass with a little bran. 1 Bucket of warm water
which was added 80 ml of sea weed solution + 1 cu
Molasses

Day	Time	Temperature of Compost / °C	Temperature Outside / °C	Tossed or Turned	Comments
1	9am	12°	12°	Turned	Dry
2	8am	42°	8°	"	added
3	9am	55	12	"	½ bucket
4	NOON	45	20	"	of water
5	8am	28	7	"	on 4th day.
6	9am	35	10	"	Note temp drop on 5th
7	9am	25	11	"	day, then
8	10am	22	8	"	rise as water absorbed.
9	11am	19	17	"	Emptied on
10					9th day

Quality of final product:

Light & Friable
Sweet Smelling
Darker yet Friable
Dark & Sticky
Sour or Rotting Odour

Dry
Moist
Soggy

Method: Tumbler
       Heap

Date Started :
Date Finished :

Method: Tumbler
       Heap
       Bin

Date Started   :
Date Finished :
Date Used   :

Location:

Where and how applied:

Composition:

Day	Time	Temperature of Compost / °C	Temperature Outside / °C	Tossed or Turned	Comments

Quality of final product:

Light & Friable
Sweet Smelling
Darker yet Friable
Dark & Sticky
Sour or Rotting Odour

Dry
Moist
Soggy

Method: Tumbler
       Heap
       Bin

Date Started   :
Date Finished :
Date Used   :

Location:

Where and how applied:

Composition:

Day	Time	Temperature of Compost / °C	Temperature Outside / °C	Tossed or Turned	Comments

Quality of final product:

Light & Friable
Sweet Smelling
Darker yet Friable
Dark & Sticky
Sour or Rotting Odour

Dry
Moist
Soggy

Method: Tumbler
       Heap
       Bin

Date Started   :
Date Finished :
Date Used   :

Location:

Where and how applied:

Composition:

Day	Time	Temperature of Compost / °C	Temperature Outside / °C	Tossed or Turned	Comments

Quality of final product:

Light & Friable   Dry
Sweet Smelling   Moist
Darker yet Friable   Soggy
Dark & Sticky
Sour or Rotting Odour

Method: Tumbler
        Heap
        Bin

Date Started   :
Date Finished :
Date Used   :

Location:

Where and how applied:

Composition:

Day	Time	Temperature of Compost / °C	Temperature Outside / °C	Tossed or Turned	Comments

Quality of final product:

Light & Friable
Sweet Smelling
Darker yet Friable
Dark & Sticky
Sour or Rotting Odour

Dry
Moist
Soggy

Method: Tumbler   Date Started   :
        Heap   Date Finished   :
        Bin   Date Used   :

Location: Where and how applied:

Composition:

Day	Time	Temperature of Compost / °C	Temperature Outside / °C	Tossed or Turned	Comments

Quality of final product:

Light & Friable   Dry
Sweet Smelling   Moist
Darker yet Friable   Soggy
Dark & Sticky
Sour or Rotting Odour

Method: Tumbler   Date Started   :
         Heap   Date Finished :
         Bin   Date Used   :

Location: Where and how applied:

Composition:

Day	Time	Temperature of Compost / °C	Temperature Outside / °C	Tossed or Turned	Comments

Quality of final product:

    Light & Friable   Dry
    Sweet Smelling   Moist
    Darker yet Friable   Soggy
    Dark & Sticky
    Sour or Rotting Odour